AWESOME MINDS

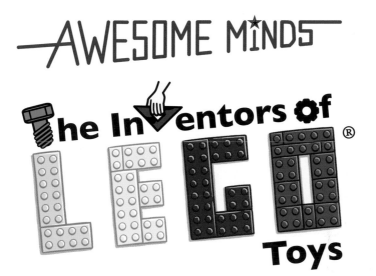

The Inventors of LEGO® Toys

By Erin Hagar

Art by Paige Garrison

duopress

We asked:

What's your favorite LEGO® memory?

Author: Erin Hagar

"A rainy summer day with my kids, building the LEGO® log cabin (Set 5766)."

Illustrator: Paige Harrison

"Leading an expedition through Space Camp with LEGO's® Space Shuttle Discovery!"

Art Director: Violet Lemay

"Watching my little boy create an entire city of tiny LEGO® skyscrapers."

Copy Chief: Michele Suchomel-Casey

"The first time I discovered LEGO® toys when I was five years old and living in Germany."

Publisher: Mauricio Velázquez de León

"Discovering that you can use the little windows to build swimming pools and other stuff."

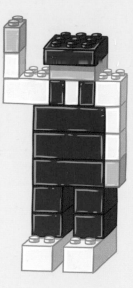

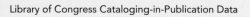

Graphic Design: Beatriz Juarez

This book is an independently authored and published
biography of the family that created the LEGO® construction
toy and is not sponsored or endorsed by or affiliated in any
way with the LEGO® Group of companies, which owns the
LEGO® trademarks. All uses of LEGO® trademarks by the
author and publisher of this book are only for the purpose
of identification, information, and commentary under the Fair
Use Doctrine, and no approval of this book by the LEGO®
Group of companies is claimed or implied.

Library of Congress Cataloging-in-Publication Data

Names: Hagar, Erin. | Garrison, Paige, illustrator.
Title: Awesome minds: the inventors of LEGO toys / by Erin Hagar; art by Paige Garrison.
Description: First Edition. | New York : Duo Press, 2016. |
Series: Awesome minds | Includes bibliographical references.
Identifiers: LCCN 2015027186| ISBN 9781938093531 (hardback) | ISBN 9781938093548 (epub)
| ISBN 9781938093555 (kindle) | ISBN 9781938093562 (PDF)
Subjects: LCSH: LEGO koncernen (Denmark)--History--Juvenile literature. | Toy industry-
-Denmark--Juvenile literature. | LEGO toys--History--Juvenile literature. | BISAC: JUVENILE
NONFICTION / Biography & Autobiography / General.
Classification: LCC HD9993.T694 H34 2016 | DDC 688.7/20922489--dc23LC
record available at http://lccn.locgov/2015027186

Printed in China
1 2 3 4 5 6 7 8 9 10
duopress
www.duopressbooks.com

Table of Contents

Billions of Bricks

This is a LEGO® brick. You can tell it's a LEGO® brick because of the studs on top and the tubes underneath. Its sturdy plastic is almost impossible to destroy. Even though the plastic is strong, you can join the bricks together and pull them apart easily—well, most of the time.

tubes

If you have a few, or a few hundred, LEGO® bricks in your house, you're not alone. Enough LEGO® bricks have been produced to give every person on Earth their own set of 86 bricks. In 2012, LEGO® factories pumped out 5.2 million bricks every hour, for a total of 45.7 billion bricks.

studs

That many bricks would wrap around Earth more than 18 times if you laid them end to end.

It's hard to imagine a world without the LEGO® brick. But like every good idea, the LEGO® brick had to be invented.

People had to work hard and risk a lot to turn this idea into a reality. Did you ever wonder who those people were?

Who invented the LEGO® brick?

● Did you know that if all the LEGO® minifigures ever created decided to form their own country, the population would be greater than the populations of China, India, the United States, Indonesia, Brazil, Pakistan, Nigeria, and Bangladesh *combined*?

LEGO® FACT

LEGO® bricks have changed very little over the years. In fact, you could mix your mom's or your dad's childhood bricks with the ones in your collection and— CLICK!—they'd snap together as though not a day had passed.

Northern Europe today

A Danish Carpenter

To answer that, let's travel back in time to Denmark, a European country that borders Germany to the north. The year is 1897. A young boy, about six years old, tends his family's sheep. His name is Ole (O-luh) Kirk Christiansen, and the story of LEGO® toys starts with him. While his sheep grazed in the fields, Ole Kirk carved

●Ole Kirk and his wife, Kirstine, had four sons— Johannes, Karl Georg, Godtfred (keep your eye on him—he's important to our story), and Gerhardt. They were a happy family.

Clockwise from left: Ole Kirk, Johannes, Kirstine, Godtfred, Gerhardt, and Karl Georg Christiansen

things out of wood with his pocketknife. He had such a talent for woodworking that his older brother, Kristian, trained him to be a professional carpenter. In 1916, when Ole Kirk was 25 years old, he bought a carpenter's shop in the farming town of Billund, not far from the village where he was born. Farmers hired Ole Kirk and his workers to build houses, dairies for the cattle, and even churches. They knew everything he built was made well.

● When Ole Kirk started his career, Billund was a small village with about 300 people. Today, the population has grown to more than 6,000. With the **LEGOLAND®** **theme park** and its bustling airport (built by the LEGO company in 1964), Billund is the second busiest tourist destination in Denmark after the country's capital, Copenhagen.

This airplane was created by an employee at the LEGOLAND® airport shop in Billund.

Ole Kirk worked hard, but things weren't easy. Farmers in Billund didn't have much money, which meant they couldn't hire Ole Kirk and his workers for many jobs.

Within a few short years, three terrible things happened to Ole Kirk and his family. First, in 1924, young Karl Georg and Godtfred accidentally set fire to a pile of wood shavings in their father's workshop. The boys were rescued, but the entire building—and their home—burned to the ground. Even though it was risky, Ole Kirk decided to rebuild. He built an even bigger workshop, and the family moved into a small apartment inside it.

To earn money, Ole Kirk decided to craft smaller items. He paid close attention to every detail, making sure all his products were of the highest quality.

TROUBLED TIMES

The economic crisis known as the Great Depression started in the United States in 1929. People who had invested money in the stock market suddenly found their investments were worth much less—or had vanished entirely. This set off a chain reaction. Banks lost millions of dollars. People couldn't afford to buy goods and services. Businesses closed, and people lost their jobs. The consequences of the Great Depression affected people all over the world.

Next, in 1929, millions of people all over the world lost their jobs. Farmers in Billund couldn't get fair prices for their crops. They stopped hiring Ole Kirk for repairs on their buildings. They couldn't afford his ironing boards and stepladders. Ole Kirk had to ask many of his workers to stop working. He just couldn't pay them.

Then, in 1932, Ole Kirk's wife died, leaving him to raise their four sons alone.

Someone else might have given up.

But Ole Kirk started to think about toys.

Almonds and Yo-yos

Toys? Yes, toys! Because even in hard times, children still play. As a father, Ole Kirk knew that parents want to make their children happy. Soon Ole Kirk's factory was producing brightly painted wooden animals, miniature cars and trucks, and piggy banks. One popular toy was a duck that quacked when you pulled it.

People liked Ole Kirk's toys, but they often couldn't afford them. Sometimes they paid with food instead of money. Ole Kirk exchanged one order of toys for a sack of almonds.

● To make his wood toys, Ole Kirk used birch trees cut from the forest. The wood dried outside for two years, then was moved to a kiln to dry for three weeks. After that, the wood could be cut and shaped into toys.

One popular game at this time was called "tipcat." To play, kids needed two sticks. A short stick was sharpened to a point on both ends. Then, using a larger stick (like a broom handle), a player would hit the small stick until it was flung up into the air. Once it was in the air, the player would swing the big stick, trying to hit the small one like a baseball.

But you can't buy materials or pay workers with almonds. Ole Kirk needed money. In 1932, he drove around Denmark, visiting his brothers and sisters to ask them for help getting a loan from the bank. They agreed, but they told him to make something more useful than toys. (Luckily for us, Ole Kirk didn't listen.)

About this time, kids all over the world were going crazy for one particular toy:

the yo-yo.

Ole Kirk's factory could barely keep up with the orders. All hours of the night, workers pushed handcarts filled with yo-yos to the train station, delivering them to toy shops around Denmark.

Then, just like that, the yo-yo craze ended. Ole Kirk had a factory full of yo-yos that nobody wanted. What a waste! Problems are for solving, Ole Kirk thought. He cut the yo-yos in half and designed a new truck that could use the yo-yos as wheels. This truck was a big seller.

Ole Kirk learned an important lesson from the yo-yo experience: Don't worry about what's popular. **Instead, make good toys that give kids new ways to play.**

●Did you know that **the yo-yo** is one of the world's oldest toys? Historians think it was first invented in China and then later introduced to places like the Philippines and Greece. There are Greek vases dating back to 500 BCE with pictures of children playing with the familiar disk and string. Astronauts have even played with yo-yos in space, researching the effects of gravity on the toy.

A Family Business

When he was just 12 years old, Godtfred started working with his father. He learned how to operate the machines in the wood shop.

He helped his father keep track of the orders and payments. Godtfred understood how important it was for the company to be careful with money. Once, while painting an order of toys, Godtfred used two coats of paint instead of the usual three. He was very proud—he'd saved the business money!

But Ole Kirk was not happy. He made Godtfred go to the train station, pick up the toys before they could be delivered, and repaint them all. Godtfred learned the hard way how serious Ole Kirk was about the company's motto: "Only the best is good enough."

By the time he was 14, Godtfred was working full-time with his father. He designed models for new toys. Ole Kirk was so impressed he gave Godtfred more responsibility in the company.

●In 1934, Ole Kirk decided to rename his company. He wanted to show how important toys were to the business. He took the Danish words for "play" and "well"—leg and godt—and combined them into the name we know today, LEGO®.

This sign with the company's motto hung at Ole Kirk's factory.

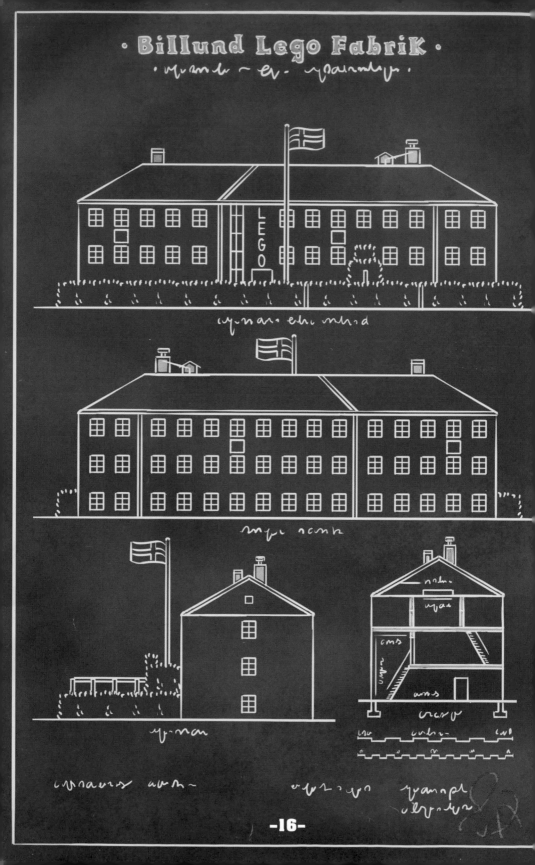

The company continued to grow. In 1942, 15 people from Billund worked for the LEGO company. That year, another fire completely destroyed the factory. By now, Ole Kirk was in his fifties, and the thought of rebuilding a second time felt over-whelming. But his employees needed him—including his four sons, who all worked for the company. Once again, Ole Kirk designed and built a new fac-tory, big enough to employ 40 workers.

With the new factory and a steady income, it would have been easy for the company to continue designing and producing well-made wooden toys. But Ole Kirk had his eye on something new plastic.

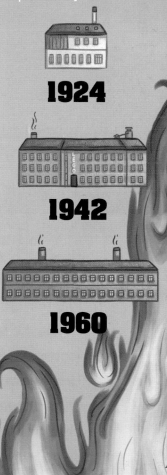

● Fires changed the LEGO company's history three times. After the fires of 1924 and 1942, the Christiansen family rebuilt their factory. After the 1960 fire, the company decided not to rebuild the old factory; they were going to focus on plastic toys instead.

1924

1942

1960

LEGO® FACT

Did you know that in Latin, the word "lego" means "I build" or "I assemble"? Ole Kirk didn't know that when he came up with the name. Wasn't that lucky, knowing the toy that would make the company famous?

The Power of Plastics

Plastic had been invented years earlier, but the use of plastic expanded during World War II. It allowed factories to produce identical items quickly and cheaply. Unlike painted wood, the color of a plastic item didn't chip or peel. Plastic was sturdy, and it was lighter and cheaper to ship.

In 1947, a salesman from a British machine company paid a visit to Billund. He wanted to sell Ole Kirk an injection-molding machine that could produce plastic toys. Even though the machine was expensive, Ole Kirk wanted to buy three of them. His family wasn't sure and convinced him to buy only one. With that purchase, the LEGO company became one of the first companies in Denmark to produce plastic goods.

Pictured here are plastic pieces from a LEGO® top set and a plastic toy window frame.

MAKING PLASTICS

Here's how the machine worked: Once the toy's design was finalized, a mold would be created out of steel or aluminum and inserted into the machine.

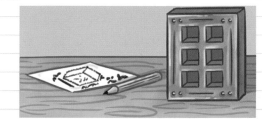

Then, plastic granules were poured into a barrel and heated to a very high temperatures.

Using great force, the molten (melted) plastic was pushed into the mold, where it would solidify into the desired shape, like cake batter baking in a pan.

Once the plastic had cooled, the pieces were ejected from the machine.

It took two years for Ole Kirk and Godtfred to get their line of plastic toys up and running. They needed to find a company to create the molds that would shape the toys. They needed another company to sell them the plastic granules to melt in the injection-molding machine. Once these pieces were in place, Godtfred designed the LEGO company's first plastic toy: a baby's rattle shaped like a fish.

Next came a plastic teddy bear flying an airplane. The company could make both of these toys in different color combinations.

Danish children loved playing with the Ferguson Trackto, a plastic tractor model the LEGO company released in 1951. Sold as a set and as individual pieces, children assembled this toy before playing with it. It was a complicated and expensive toy to produce, but the investment paid off and the Trackto sold well.

SAMLESÆT TIL *Ferguson* MODEL TRAKTOR

FREMSTILLET AF LEGO DANMARK

The Trackto taught Ole Kirk and Godtfred an important lesson: Children enjoyed building the toys **they would play with.**

• The LEGO company sold the Automatic Binding Bricks as gift sets to toy stores around Denmark starting in 1949. But the bricks didn't sell very well, and many boxes were sent back to the factory unopened. A writer for a Danish toy magazine toured the LEGO® factory in Billund and wrote, "Plastics will never take the place of good, solid wooden toys."

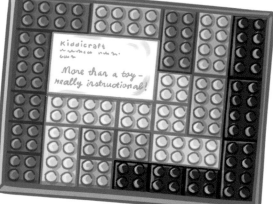

The first set of LEGO® Automatic Binding Bricks (1949)

Kiddicrafts's Self-Locking Building Blocks, released in 1947

The Automatic Binding Brick

The LEGO company had been making wooden blocks for years. Now, with his injection-molding machine, Ole Kirk started to think about plastic blocks. He wasn't the first toy maker with this idea. In fact, the salesman who sold Ole Kirk

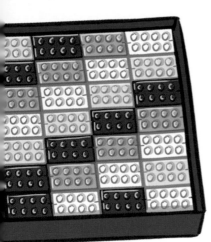

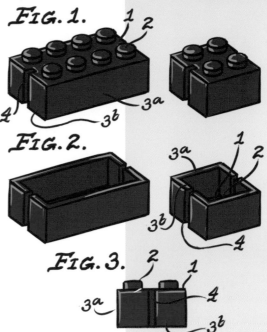

FIG. 1.

FIG. 2.

FIG. 3.

●Hollow underneath, the Automatic Binding Bricks came in two sizes (one with four studs and one with eight studs) and four colors (red, green, white, and yellow). The bricks had slits in the sides to hold the window and door pieces that were also part of the set. The LEGO company was still perfecting its plastic production. Sometimes extra plastic from the mold would get stuck in the slits.

the injection-molding machine gave him a sample of a hollow, plastic brick made by the British company Kiddicraft. After making a few minor changes to the sample, Ole Kirk and Godtfred released the LEGO company's first plastic blocks, the Automatic Binding Bricks.

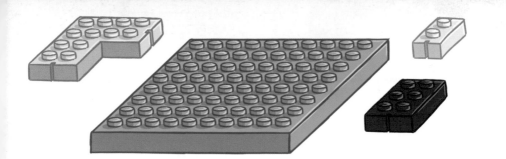

By 1951, Ole Kirk's health began to suffer. Godtfred, just 30 years old, found himself in charge of the LEGO company's operations. There was a lot to do. He had to raise money to build a new, modern factory for the company's 140 workers. Those workers produced more than 200 types of LEGO® toys in both wood and plastic (or a combination of the two).

Many of the plastic toys were selling well, but not the Automatic Binding Bricks. To make the bricks more appealing, Godtfred changed the name to LEGO® Mursten (LEGO® "bricks") and created sets around certain themes, like houses. He also designed more styles of bricks, such as the 1x2 and 2x3 bricks, corner pieces, and a base plate for children to build on. Still, not many children played with the sets.

● Ole Kirk and Godtfred argued about the new factory. Godtfred thought it was too expensive and didn't want to build it. But Ole Kirk insisted, telling his son to find the money. Godtfred was so upset that he almost left the company for good! The two men made up, the factory was built, and Godtfred helped the company to grow bigger than ever.

The Idea
That Changed
Everything

A few years later, while traveling to Britain to attend a toy fair, Godtfred chatted with a fellow traveler on the ferry. This man was an expert in toys and sales. He chose the toys department stores would sell to customers. Their conversation—actually, one word in the conversation—changed the LEGO company forever. That word?

" SYSTEM "

What you need, the man told Godtfred, is a toy that is part of a bigger system, something that connects one set of toys to another.

Children could add new pieces to their collections, making the toy different each time they played.

A system. Godtfred could not get this idea out of his head.

A BIG SHOW AND TELL!

A toy fair is an exhibition organized so that companies in the toy industry can introduce and demonstrate their latest products under the same roof. Toy fairs are held all over the world, but the most important are organized in New York, USA, Nuremberg, Germany, and London, England.

A System

When he returned to Billund, Godtfred challenged himself to create a LEGO® system of play. What traits should a system have, he wondered?
He came up with 10:

10 IMPORTANT LEGO FEATURES

1. LEGO = unlimited play potential
2. LEGO = for girls, for boys
3. LEGO = fun for every age
4. LEGO = year-round play
5. LEGO = healthy and quiet play
6. LEGO = long hours of play
7. LEGO = development, imagination, creativity
8. LEGO = the more LEGO, the greater its value
9. LEGO = extra sets available
10. LEGO = quality in every detail

With these traits in mind, Godtfred considered every toy—more than 200 in all—that his company produced. The best fit? The LEGO® Mursten, or LEGO® brick. It was a risky idea. At the time, LEGO® bricks made up only a small portion of the company's sales, about 5 to 10 percent.

● By the mid-1950s, many manufacturers, such as American Bricks, Bayko, Lincoln Logs, and Minibrix, were selling architectural toys, but none of these toys formed a system. Using the brick as part of a fully integrated system was the idea that set the LEGO company apart from the others.

• Godtfred and his team added accessories to bring the town to life— things like miniature trees, vehicles, and street signs. Gradually, people started buying more sets in Denmark and, soon after, in neighboring countries like Sweden, Norway, and Germany.

Clutch Power

If the system was going to work, Godtfred had to make some improvements. First, he asked his employees to create sets of LEGO® bricks around particular themes. Their first theme was the Town Plan, with sets designed to build houses, factories, and shops.

• How did the winning design work? The studs on top of one brick fit between the round tubes and the side-walls underneath a second brick. Friction kept the two bricks connected, but they could be easily broken apart again. Godtfred called this ability "clutch power," and it's the same design used in LEGO® bricks today.

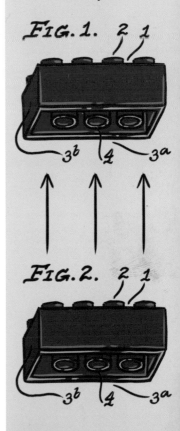

FIG. 1. 2 1

3b 4 3a

FIG. 2. 2 1

3b 4 3a

Second, Godtfred needed to improve the brick itself. Children complained that the structures made with the hollow bricks collapsed easily and couldn't be moved when they were finished. Godtfred and his team designed several new models of bricks that attached together. They tried out their designs with groups of children and, in 1958, they settled on the winner.

This brick—what Godtfred called the "real" LEGO®
brick—changed the company forever. Now combinations
of bricks could be put together in hundreds, thousands,
millions of ways. New styles of bricks were possible, like
the sloping roofs to make more realistic buildings. Children
could build anything they could imagine.

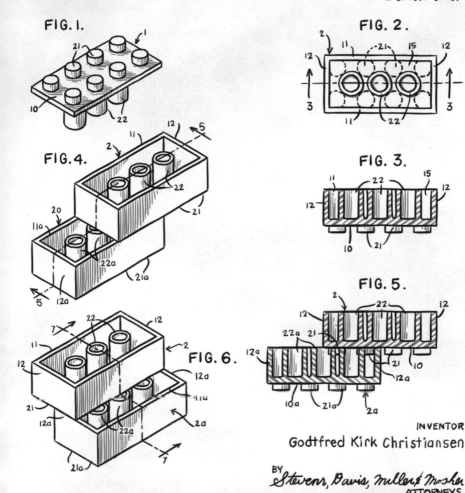

FIG. 1.

FIG. 2.

FIG. 3.

FIG.4.

FIG. 5.

FIG. 6.

INVENTOR

Godtfred Kirk Christiansen

BY Stevens, Davis, Miller & Mosher

ATTORNEYS

Godtfred knew how important this design was to the LEGO company, so he wrote an application for a patent.

On January 28, 1958, Godtfred presented his application to the patent office in Copenhagen, Denmark. Later, he applied for patents in all the countries where the LEGO® bricks were sold.

- A patent is a legal protection for an invention. Receiving a patent meant that only the LEGO company would be allowed to make, use, or sell toys with this stud-and-tube design for a certain number of years.

Thank You, Ole Kirk!

Sadly, Ole Kirk Christiansen never saw the LEGO® brick that would become so important to his company. On March 11, 1958, Ole Kirk died after several years of poor health. He was 67 years old. A year before his death, however, Ole Kirk enjoyed the LEGO company's 25th birthday party, a huge celebration of everything Ole Kirk had done for Billund and his employees.

●As a carpenter, Ole Kirk built houses, churches, and other buildings for the people of Billund. As a businessman, he continued to put his community first. When his factory burned in 1942, he turned down invitations to move his company to other parts of Denmark. Instead, he stayed with the people and town he called home. Ole Kirk bought land near the new factory and used it to provide affordable homes for his employees. To show its appreciation, the town named a street after him!

With the newly designed LEGO® brick in place, Godtfred made big changes to the company. First, he stopped making most of the plastic toys that were not part of the LEGO® brick system. In fact, by 1958 the LEGO® bricks were the only plastic toys the company made.

Second, Godtfred divided the company into two parts. The LEGO® division would make the bricks, and the second division—named Bilofix—would make the wood toys. Bilofix would be managed by Godtfred's brother Gerhardt.

But the future of the Bilofix division would be cut short. In 1960, yet another fire destroyed the warehouse of wood toys, ruining the entire inventory of toys inside. Godtfred decided not to rebuild the warehouse and to stop making wooden toys all together. For a toy company that started with wood toys, this was a big decision.

Not everyone agreed. Soon after, Godtfred's brothers Gerhardt and Karl Georg decided to leave the LEGO company for good.

Some examples of the toys produced in the 1960s, like the LEGO® System Supplementary Set (left) and the brick house and scooter from the LEGO® Town Plan Set (top and left)

A British advertisement and a LEGO® mascot from the 1960s

System im Spiel

The traffic sign (above left) was part of the 1960s Supplementary Set. Above right, a German advertisement from the same era draws attention to the LEGO® system.

• Another popular toy came on the scene in the 1960s—the modeling clay known as Play-Doh®. The squishy substance actually started out as a wallpaper cleaner. When the manufacturer realized it had made a nontoxic clay that was easy to clean up, it was quickly packaged as a toy and sold to schools and toy stores. More than 700 million pounds of Play-Doh® have been sold over the years. That's the power of innovation!

Rolling Forward

Now that LEGO® bricks were the company's only product, Godtfred had to think hard about what products he added to the system. He hired a team of five workers to develop and test new ideas. He called this team LEGO® Futura. During the 1960s, as the LEGO company introduced itself to kids around the world, the Futura group created many innovations still in use today. Here are a few you'll recognize for sure!

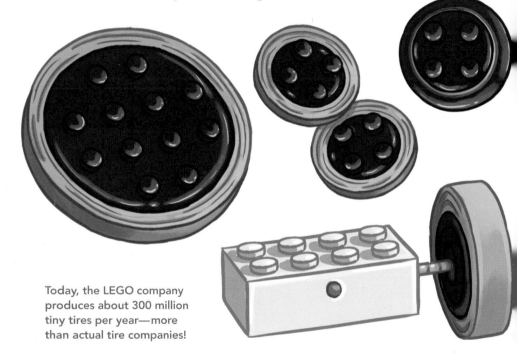

Today, the LEGO company produces about 300 million tiny tires per year—more than actual tire companies!

• The LEGO® wheel, which got its very own patent. With the wheel, children could build their own movable LEGO® creations. The wheels were made with a round brick that had a groove to hold a rubber tire. A modified 2x4 brick held the axle, allowing the wheel to spin freely.

• The wordless instruction sheets, which use visual cues and illustrations to show a LEGO® set assembled brick by brick. It's a system still used by the LEGO company—and other toy companies—today.

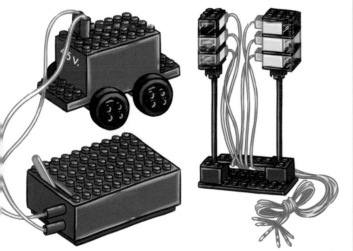

• A motorized system that allowed children to build a functioning toy train. The motorized components would later inspire the LEGO® TECHNIC series.

• Plastic is the material on which the LEGO company is built. However, plastics are not great for the environment, and the LEGO company hopes to eliminate their use altogether in the next few years. The company has already reduced the amount of plastic in its packaging and is now looking for more environmentally friendly material for the bricks themselves. It won't be easy. The bricks still need to click with earlier bricks and should be strong enough to last for generations. But the LEGO Group recognizes the need to reduce its carbon footprint and is committed to creating a more sustainable toy for a better planet.

As LEGO offices opened up throughout Europe in the early 1960s, Godtfred and his team needed easier ways to travel. They bought a small airplane that took off from a field near Billund. Sometimes LEGO employees had to drive to the field and turn on their car headlights so the pilot could see the landing area. Eventually, the company built an airstrip and convinced neighboring towns to operate it as a public airport. Today, the Billund airport is the second busiest in Denmark, in large part because of LEGOLAND® visitors.

In 1966, Godtfred cleared a large section of land between the factory and the Billund airport to build the park. This was still a remote area of Denmark. Would the investment pay off? Would people come to LEGOLAND®?

Yes, indeed! On the park's first day, June 7, 1968, about 3,000 people showed up. By the end of that summer, LEGOLAND® had welcomed more than 625,000 visitors. Godtfred never dreamed the park would be so popular.

LEGOLAND®

By the mid-1960s, more than 20,000 people toured the LEGO® factory every year. Schoolchildren and adults loved looking at the large models the design team created for department stores and toy fairs.

All those people trudging through his factory made Godtfred grouchy. He wondered about an outdoor exhibit of LEGO® designs.

"What I had in mind first," Godtfred remembered later, "was something in the way of a large open-air show, maybe the size of a football field, where a [retired] couple could sell tickets and perhaps run a small cafeteria."

Well, like most things at the LEGO company, imagination took over and LEGOLAND® was born. Designers planned a 3-acre park where visitors could stroll past LEGO® models of familiar European landmarks, ride a large LEGO® train, and practice driving in a "traffic school." Of course, there was an open area where children could create their own LEGO® creations, too.

● Godtfred's cousin, Dagny Holm, was a professional sculptor. As a young woman, she designed some of Ole Kirk's wooden toys. Later, she began "sculpting" LEGO® models on a scale larger than the company had been using. Dagny became the chief LEGO® designer, and she oversaw the models that would fill LEGOLAND®—more than six million bricks in all!

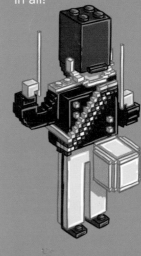

Kjeld, C.E.O   '79

A New Generation

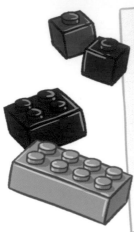

If anybody can say that he "grew up" with LEGO® bricks, that person is Kjeld Kirk Kristiansen, Godtfred's son and Ole Kirk's grandson. As a boy, Kjeld tested new LEGO® designs and instruction manuals before they were available to the public. The company used a photo of Kjeld on the boxes of early LEGO® sets, like the 1959 Town Plan.

As a young man, Kjeld worked for the LEGO Company in Germany and Switzerland. He played a big role in establishing the company's American sales office. In 1977, Kjeld went back to Billund and joined the management team.

This was an exciting time in the LEGO company's history. DUPLO®, oversized bricks for preschoolers, had hit the market. New LEGO® sets and themes—

like Space and Town and Castle—were selling all over the world. Those sets were even more exciting because they included that familiar yellow LEGO® minifigure we know today. While Kjeld didn't invent the minifigure himself, he knew how important it would be for the company because it "added the human touch and the role play element to the LEGO® play experience."

But this was also a difficult time for the company. Sales were down. All these new product lines and ideas were challenging to manage. When he was just 31 years old, Kjeld became president of the company and created what he called a "system within the system." He divided the main LEGO® products into three categories: DUPLO®, the construction toys, and a third category for other kinds of LEGO® play material, like the LEGO® jewelry-making kits known as SCALA®. This new structure allowed LEGO employees to be more creative and flexible when designing toys within the categories.

● Under Kjeld's leadership, the company experienced a 15-year growth spurt, doubling in size every five years. In 2000, both *Fortune* magazine and the British Association of Toy Retailers named the LEGO® brick the "Toy of the Century."

● DUPLO® got its name because the bricks are exactly double the size of traditional LEGO® bricks. Even with the size difference, they still "click" with LEGO® bricks.

Billions of Hours

Today, LEGO® bricks are some of the world's most popular toys. But they're so much more. Businesses use LEGO® bricks to help their employees think more creatively. Artists like Nathan Sawaya use LEGO® bricks to make amazing sculptures exhibited all over the world. Educators have used LEGO® products to challenge students in math and science. In 2015, a team of Girl Scouts wondered how they could make reading easier for people who can't move their arms. They designed a battery-powered page-turning machine built from LEGO® bricks and LEGO® tires. They won the White House Science Fair and got to meet the president of the United States!

But perhaps the most amazing thing about LEGO® toys is the way they have seeped into our culture, allowing us to create mini-worlds of the books, movies, comic books, and video games that we love.

When Ole Kirk and Godtfred Christiansen designed that first hollow brick, they had no idea how a tiny piece of plastic would change the world. It didn't happen overnight, but the LEGO® company turned that brick into a toy that gets more than five billion hours of playtime every year. Getting there took determination, hard work, and most of all, imagination.

You know that crashing, clacking sound you hear when hundreds of LEGO® bricks are dumped on the floor? That's the sound of possibilities, the sound of your own imagination gearing up to combine those bricks into anything you want. There are billions of things those LEGO® bricks can be.

What will you build?

"Not until that day when I said to myself, 'You must make a choice between carpentry and toys,' did I find the real answer. **As it turned out, it was the right decision."**

—Ole Kirk Christiansen

GLOSSARY

carbon footprint The negative environmental impact a person or company creates when using fossil fuels.

innovation The introduction of something new.

invest To put out money in the hopes of making more money.

kiln An oven or furnace for hardening or drying something.

loan Money borrowed (usually from a bank) that must be repaid, often with an additional fee.

motto A short phrase describing the beliefs or ideals of an institution.

population The number of people living in a country or region.

stock A unit of share in a company that is purchased and sold by investors, hopefully for a profit.

trait A quality or characteristic of someone or something.

READ MORE ABOUT INVENTORS

Abdul-Jabbar, Kareem, Raymond Obstfeld, Ben Boos, and AG Ford. *What Color Is My World?: The Lost History of African-American Inventors*. Somerville, MA: Candlewick, 2012.

Barton, Chris, and Tony Persiani. *The Day-Glo Brothers: The True Story of Bob and Joe Switzer's Bright Ideas and Brand-new Colors*. Watertown, MA: Charlesbridge, 2009.

Davis, Kathryn, and Gilbert Ford. *Mr. Ferris and His Wheel*. Boston: Houghton Mifflin, 2014.

McCarthy, Meghan. *Pop!: The Invention of Bubble Gum*. New York: Simon & Schuster for Young Readers, 2010.

Thimmesh, Catherine, and Melissa Sweet. *Girls Think of Everything: Stories of Ingenious Inventions by Women*. Boston: Houghton Mifflin, 2000.

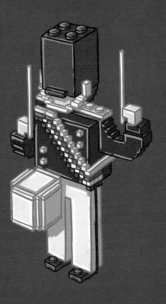

INDEX